INTRODUCTION

Young Jane Goodall had big dreams. She wanted to work with wild animals in Africa. But in the 1940s, women did not become animal scientists or go on dangerous adventures.

Jane did not let that stop her. At the age of twenty-six, she went to live in the forests of the modern-day country of Tanzania, in eastern Africa. There, she studied chimpanzees. She became the world's first chimpanzee expert.

In 1986, Jane learned that chimps were in danger of dying out. Since then, she has traveled around the world. She teaches people about protecting wild chimpanzees and caring for our planet. She believes that each one of us can make a difference.

This is her story.

1 ANIMAL LOVER

Valerie Jane Morris-Goodall was born in London, England, on April 3, 1934. Animals fascinated her from the start. Valerie Jane's parents, Mortimer and Vanne Morris-Goodall, encouraged her love of animals. Her father gave her a stuffed animal chimpanzee when she was a baby. It was called Jubilee. Jubilee quickly became Valerie Jane's favorite toy. She carried it everywhere with her.

In 1939, the Morris-Goodalls left London with five-year-old Valerie Jane and her baby sister, Judy. They moved into the home of Vanne's mother, Elizabeth Joseph. She lived in the town of Bournemouth. Young Valerie Jane had trouble saying "Granny." So she called her grandmother Danny. Soon everyone else did too.

This travel poster from the 1930s shows the town of Bournemouth. The city's location by the sea made it attractive to visitors.

BOURNEMOUTH
The Centre of Health & Pleasure
Guide Book free from Publicity Manager, Town Hall, Bournemouth.
TRAVEL BY L M S "PINES" EXPRESS FROM THE NORTH & MIDLANDS

Valerie Jane liked living in Danny's large brick house. She was allowed to keep all kinds of pets there. She had cats, guinea pigs, tortoises, and other animals. But Valerie Jane's favorite pet was her dog, Rusty.

Valerie Jane also had a strong curiosity about animals in nature. She spent many hours in her grandmother's big backyard and garden. She liked to hide in secret places behind bushes or in trees. From there, she watched birds making their nests. She saw spiders spinning their webs. She spied rabbits, foxes, and weasels.

Jane's favorite pet, Rusty, was a black spaniel mix like this dog.

LIKE FATHER, LIKE DAUGHTER

Jane's father risked his life to fight in World War II (1939–1945). Then he remained in the British army for several years after the war. Jane did not see much of her father during that time. But he showed her the importance of having courage. He also passed on to her his love of adventure.

On rainy days, Valerie Jane read inside. One of her favorite books was *Tarzan of the Apes*. She loved the stories about Tarzan, a man who grew up in the African jungle. Valerie Jane daydreamed about living in the wild like Tarzan. She wanted to have adventures in Africa. Most of all, she wanted to live among the animals. When she grew up, she planned to make her dream come true.

Many people would have thought Valerie Jane's dream was impossible. In the 1940s, most women got married and settled down. They didn't go on adventures in the wild.

But Valerie Jane's family believed in her. Vanne especially encouraged her daughter to follow her dreams. She said, "If you really want something, and you work hard enough . . . and never give up, you will find a way."

Valerie Jane's parents divorced when she was twelve years old. But in many ways, her life stayed the same. She, Judy, and her mother still lived with her grandmother. And she continued to dream about going to Africa.

Jane liked living in Bournemouth (BELOW) at her grandmother's house, the Birches.

When Jane was young, some women worked in sewing factories such as this one. Others trained to be secretaries.

By the time Valerie Jane finished high school, she was just called Jane. Several years later, Jane also started simply using Goodall as her last name.

Jane wanted to study at a university. But her family didn't have enough money to pay for it. Jane's mother suggested that she become a secretary. Secretaries could get jobs anywhere, her mother told her, even in Africa. Nineteen-year-old Jane took her mother's advice. She trained and worked as a secretary in London. In her free time, she took free classes. She also read lots of books and went to museums. She wanted to make sure she kept learning new things.

One day in 1956, Jane got a letter from an old school friend. Her name was Clo Mange. Clo's family had just moved to the African country of Kenya. She asked if Jane would like to visit. Jane was thrilled. She responded right away: Yes! She would come as soon as possible, she told Clo. After several months, Jane had saved up enough money for the journey.

Jane was leaving behind her home and family for a faraway place. She did not know what she would find in Africa. But she knew it would be the adventure of a lifetime.

2 ADVENTURE IN AFRICA

In March 1957, Jane boarded a ship sailing for Africa. She spent several exciting weeks with Clo's family in Kenya. She talked with them about her dream of working with African animals. Someone told her to visit a man named Louis Leakey.

Louis Leakey was a famous scientist. In Africa, he had found bones and tools from the earliest humans.

LOUIS LEAKEY

Before Louis Leakey, scientists believed that humans came from Asia or Europe. Louis disagreed. He was sure that the first people lived in Africa. He spent many years trying to prove it. In Africa, he dug deep below the earth. He found old bones and skulls from millions of years ago. These ancient remains, or fossils, had been buried over time. Some of them were older than fossils found anywhere else in the world. Louis's discoveries proved that the first humans did live in Africa.

Louis was also interested in the great apes. Those include gorillas, orangutans, and chimpanzees.

Louis Leakey agreed to meet with Jane. She loved hearing him talk about his work. And her knowledge of Africa impressed him. He decided to hire her as his secretary.

Jane worked with Louis for more than a year. She learned more about Africa's wildlife and ancient past from him. He became a good teacher and friend.

After a while, Louis began talking to Jane about his interest in chimpanzees. These intelligent animals live in Africa. They are more like humans than any other animal. But people knew very little about them at the time.

Most animal scientists had only studied chimpanzees in zoos. Very few had tried to learn about chimps in nature. And even those scientists had spent only a few weeks or months in the wild. Louis wanted to find someone who would study wild chimp-anzees for much longer.

In the 1950s, people didn't know very much about wild chimps.

Louis told Jane how difficult the job would be. He had to find just the right person to do it—someone who was adventurous and fearless. Louis needed someone who wouldn't mind living among wild animals. Some of the animals would be dangerous.

Jane learned a lot about Africa's wildlife from Louis Leakey.

Louis also told Jane that the job would take a lot of patience and hard work. It would mean closely watching the chimpanzees for many hours.

Each time Louis talked about the project, Jane felt sad. The job sounded perfect for her. But she had no training. She hadn't even studied at a university. She thought he would never choose her.

Finally, she told him, "Louis, I wish you wouldn't keep talking about it because that's just what I want to do." Louis smiled. He said he was glad to hear that. Because he wanted to give the job to her.

Jane could hardly believe her luck. She was going to live out her childhood dream. She couldn't wait to get started.

3 LIFE WITH THE CHIMPANZEES

Louis wanted Jane to study chimpanzees in the Gombe Stream Chimpanzee Reserve. This hilly forest was in the modern-day country of Tanzania.

Jane arrived in Gombe around July 14, 1960. Her mother had come too. Vanne planned to help Jane get started. Jane had also hired someone to help with cooking and other chores.

The first day, Jane and Vanne set up their tent. Then Jane went off to explore. Green, leafy trees covered the steep hills of the forest. Swift streams flowed across the land. Leopards, baboons, and poisonous snakes roamed the area.

Jane climbed up the nearest slope and looked around. She saw a blue sky. She heard the sound of birds. She smelled ripe fruit growing in the trees.

This map shows the location of Gombe in Tanzania, where Jane studied chimps. Gombe became a national park in 1968.

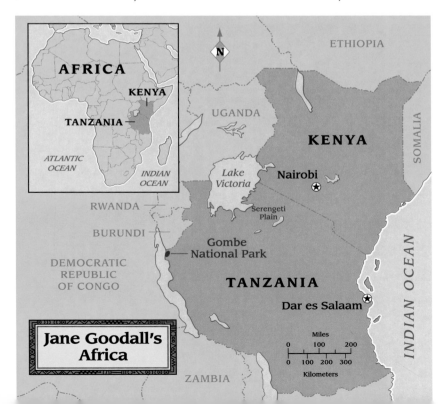

When Jane first got to Gombe, she couldn't find many chimpanzees to study.

This was the place Jane had been dreaming about since childhood. Already it felt like home. That first night, she slept outside of her tent, underneath the stars.

Jane spent the next weeks searching for chimpanzees. She always carried binoculars and a small notepad. She wanted to write down everything she saw the chimpanzees do. But she had trouble finding any chimpanzees at all.

Sometimes Jane did see a few chimps. But they always ran away from her. They seemed to be very frightened of people.

Jane knew she would never be able to learn about them unless she could get closer to them. Somehow, she had to earn the chimpanzees' trust. She just didn't know how to do it.

One day, Jane discovered a rocky lookout on the slope near her camp. From there, she could look down into the valley. She saw more chimpanzees that day than ever before. They didn't run away from her, either. They knew she was too far up to harm them.

Jane named her new lookout the Peak. She walked up to it early each morning. Often, she sat on the Peak all day. The chimpanzees got used to seeing her there. They became a little less afraid of her.

Jane watches chimpanzees from her lookout on the Peak.

Sometimes Jane left the Peak to follow a group of chimpanzees. She pushed her way through the dense forest. She struggled up and down hills. She waded through streams. She even climbed up trees. But she always stayed far behind the chimpanzees. And the moment they seemed frightened of her, she left them alone.

Jane began to discover how much the chimpanzees were like people. They hugged and kissed their friends and family. They held hands and patted one another. They teased and tickled. When they were mad, they punched, kicked, and pinched.

Jane found that chimps act a lot like people do with their families.

This chimp is using a twig as a tool.

In November, Jane made another discovery. She learned that the chimpanzees could make grass and twigs into tools. They picked blades of grass or pulled leaves off twigs to dig for termites. Those insects are a tasty chimpanzee treat.

Until then, scientists believed that only humans used tools. Jane's discovery proved that wrong. It also changed the way scientists thought about the difference between animals and humans.

Jane sits with David Greybeard. He was the first Gombe chimp to become friendly with her.

Vanne left Gombe soon after Jane's big discovery. Jane missed her mother. But she also enjoyed being on her own. She felt more and more at home in the peace of the forest.

Jane continued to spend each day studying the chimpanzees. The animals began to let her get closer to them. And Jane started to see that each chimpanzee had its own personality. They also seemed to have their own thoughts and feelings, like people. Jane gave the chimps names, such as David Greybeard, Flo, and Gilka. She also began to care about them as friends.

Jane wrote to Louis about everything she was learning. He wanted her to share her discoveries with other scientists. But most scientists did not take her work seriously. Almost all animal scientists were men. They didn't think a young woman like Jane could study chimpanzees properly. She hadn't even gone to college, they pointed out.

Jane decided to solve that problem. Starting in 1962, she spent part of each year in England. She studied at Cambridge University there. She planned to get an advanced degree in ethology. Ethologists study how animals behave.

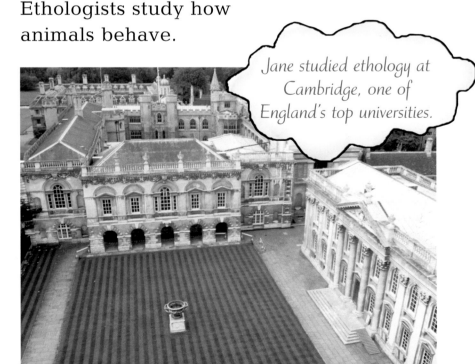

Jane studied ethology at Cambridge, one of England's top universities.

Chimpanzee Facts

- There are probably around 150,000 wild chimpanzees on Earth. They live in Africa.

- They can live forty to fifty years in the wild.

- They are usually 3 to 5 feet tall. Females weigh around 70 to 100 pounds. Males weigh around 90 to 120 pounds.

- Chimpanzees often remain close to family members all their lives. They also keep close friendships.

- They live together in communities of about forty or fifty chimpanzees. Each community lives on its own area of land.

- They use a mixture of sounds, motions, and facial expressions to communicate.

But many of Jane's teachers at Cambridge did not respect her work either. They did not believe that animals could have different personalities. They also did not believe that chimpanzees could have thoughts or feelings.

Jane's teachers told her not to give the chimpanzees names. They told her not to care so much about the animals. But she refused to change.

Jane knew that her way of working with the chimpanzees was good. After all, she had already learned more about them than any other person. She had become a chimpanzee expert.

4 CHIMPANZEE EXPERT

Jane returned to Gombe in the summer of 1962, between school years. She continued to learn more about the chimpanzees. The animals also grew to trust her more. Some of them even began coming to her camp. They took bananas from her. They let her touch them or hold their hand. Best of all, they let Jane watch them closely day after day.

During that time, a photographer came to work with Jane. *National Geographic* magazine had hired him. The magazine wanted to publish an article about Jane's work.

The photographer's name was Hugo van Lawick. He was a smart and handsome young man from the Netherlands. He loved being in nature as much as Jane did. They worked well together. And they enjoyed each other's company.

This is one of the photos Hugo van Lawick took of Jane.

The *National Geographic* article about Jane came out the next summer. It was called "My Life Among Wild Chimpanzees." Millions of people read about the twenty-nine-year-old chimpanzee expert. They saw Hugo's photographs of Jane and the chimpanzees she had grown to love.

Jane had also fallen in love with Hugo. They married on March 24, 1964. Hugo came to live with Jane in Gombe. Together, they started the Gombe Stream Research Center.

A curious helper climbs on Hugo's camera as he takes photos with Jane.

Jane became famous in the 1960s for her work with chimpanzees.

Jane invited scientists and university students to the research center. She wanted to teach them her way of studying chimpanzees. She hoped they could help her observe and learn more about the animals.

The next year, Jane received her PhD degree from Cambridge. She had become quite famous by then. In 1965, she was on the cover of *National Geographic*. She also appeared in two television shows about chimpanzees.

Jane's work fascinated people. They loved learning about her experiences with wild chimpanzees. Jane also inspired other young women to become animal scientists.

Jane's work as a scientist kept her busy, but in 1967 she became a mother too. On March 4, Jane gave birth to a baby boy. She and Hugo named him Hugo Eric Louis. But they soon called him by his nickname, Grub.

Jane and Hugo lived with Grub in Gombe, which became a national park in 1968. The family also spent a lot of time on the Serengeti, a large wilderness area in northern Tanzania. It is home to animals such as zebras, lions, and cheetahs.

(LEFT TO RIGHT) Jane, Grub, and Hugo lived at Gombe.

Lions and gazelles are two animals found in the Serengeti. Jane studied animals of the Serengeti with Hugo.

Hugo was working on a film and a book about the Serengeti. Jane helped him by studying some of the animals there. She also helped him write the book. It was published in 1970.

Jane published her own book the next year. *In the Shadow of Man* described her work in Gombe. The book became a best-seller. It inspired her to write other books for adults and children.

Jane at Gombe, playing with an eleven-month-old chimp named Flint

In 1971, Jane also began teaching at Stanford University in California. She worked there for part of the year. The rest of the year she lived in Africa. She helped to run her research center at Gombe.

Jane was always happy to return to the chimpanzees and the peace of the forest. But Hugo was away from Gombe more and more. His work took him to other parts of Africa. When he and Jane were together, they often fought. They decided to divorce in 1974.

Around that time, Jane fell in love with another man. His name was Derek Bryceson. Derek was British. But he had lived in Tanzania for years. He was in charge of the country's national parks. He was also one of Tanzania's elected lawmakers.

Jane married Derek in 1975. She happily settled into her new life with him. During the summers, Grub was also with them at Gombe. He visited during his break from school in Britain.

Derek and Jane married in 1975.

THE JANE GOODALL INSTITUTE

In 1977, some American friends helped Jane start a new organization. They called it the Jane Goodall Institute for Wildlife Research, Education and Conservation. The institute has supported Jane's work with chimpanzees. It also works to protect chimpanzees and the places where they live. And it encourages people to take better care of the environment.

In 1980, Jane and Derek received some bad news. Derek had cancer. They went to doctors in Europe to find a cure. Jane did everything she could to help. Nothing worked. Derek died that October.

Derek's death filled Jane with sadness and despair. She could not imagine living without him. She knew of only one place that would help her heal: Gombe.

5 MAKING A DIFFERENCE

The peace of Gombe soothed Jane. Its sights, sounds, and smells calmed her. And time with the chimpanzees helped her leave some of her sadness behind. Slowly, she returned to her work.

Jane had been studying chimpanzees for more than twenty years. She had learned so much about her great ape friends. She wanted to share that knowledge with other scientists.

In 1986, Jane published *The Chimpanzees of Gombe*. This scientific book earned Jane great respect from other animal scientists.

Jane had changed the way many scientists studied chimpanzees and other wild animals. Like Jane, these scientists had begun to observe the animals closely. They learned how the animals lived day by day. They came to know the personality of each animal.

Jane taught scientists how to study chimps by getting to know each one.

Many forests in Africa have been cut down, leaving many chimps with no place to live.

In November 1986, Jane went to a conference with other chimpanzee experts. They gathered to honor her for her work. They also wanted to share their knowledge with one another.

Some scientists talked about the problems facing chimpanzees. They said that chimpanzees were in danger of becoming extinct, or dying out.

Jane learned that chimpanzees were losing their forest homes. Many forests in Africa had been cut down. People used the wood to build homes. They grew crops on the land. But chimpanzees could not survive with so few places left to live.

Even the chimpanzees that did survive had problems. Hunters wanted to kill them for their meat. Other people stole baby chimpanzees from the forest. They sold them to circuses or to people as pets. These chimpanzees often lived lonely, unhappy lives.

Jane also learned that some chimpanzees had been sold to medical labs. Medical scientists experimented on the animals. They hoped to find cures for human diseases. But labs were not good homes for the chimpanzees. The animals spent their lives alone in small cages.

Jane was worried about chimpanzees that were sold to circuses.

Jane wanted to protect the animals she had spent her life studying.

All of this information shocked Jane. She decided to leave her study of chimpanzees to younger scientists. Instead, she wanted to spend the rest of her life helping her animal friends.

Jane began meeting with government leaders in Africa. She asked them to stop people from cutting down forests. She asked them to make it illegal to hunt or sell chimpanzees. She also helped to rescue chimpanzees that had been stolen from the forest.

In the United States, Jane visited medical labs. She worked with medical scientists to improve conditions for chimpanzees. She also talked about her wish to someday end animal experiments altogether.

Over time, Jane has added to the focus of her work. Like many people, she is worried about our planet. She believes that humans have harmed Earth. She teaches children and adults about protecting the planet from future harm.

AWARD WINNER

Jane has won many awards for her work. These honors have come from countries such as Tanzania, Japan, France, and the United States. In April 2002, the United Nations also honored Jane. This international organization works to improve life for people around the world. The United Nations chose Jane to be one of its Messengers of Peace. Her job is to help ordinary people work to make the world a better place.

Jane gives Kofi Annan, former head of the United Nations, a stuffed monkey. Jane often meets with world leaders to talk about how to help chimpanzees.

Jane spends most of her time traveling around the world. She asks people to help care for the planet, its animals, and one another. She believes that each person can make a difference.

Jane doesn't spend much time in Gombe anymore. But the forest and chimpanzees are never far. She carries memories of them with her wherever she goes.

TIMELINE

In the year . . .

1939   Jane moved with her family from London to Bournemouth, England.
World War II began. Jane's father joined the fighting.

1946   her parents got divorced.   `Age 12`

1954   she got her first job as a secretary.

1957   she arrived in Kenya and met Louis Leakey.   `Age 23`

1960   she began to study chimpanzees at the Gombe Stream Chimpanzee Reserve.

1963   *National Geographic* magazine published its first article about Jane.   `Age 29`

1964   she married Hugo van Lawick on March 28.
she started the Gombe Stream Research Center.

1965   she finished her PhD in ethology at Cambridge University.

1967   her son, Hugo "Grub," was born.

1971   she published *In the Shadow of Man*.   `Age 37`

1974   she and Hugo divorced.

1975   she married Derek Bryceson.   `Age 40`

1977   the Jane Goodall Institute formed.

1980   her husband, Derek, died of cancer.

1986   she published *The Chimpanzees of Gombe*.   `Age 52`
she began working to protect chimpanzees.

1991   she helped start Roots and Shoots.

2002   she was named a United Nations Messenger of Peace.   `Age 68`

2006   she received awards for her life's work from the president of France and from the Disney Wildlife Conservation Fund.

ROOTS AND SHOOTS

Jane Goodall believes that children have the power to make a big difference in the world. In 1991, she helped start an organization just for them. It is called Roots and Shoots. Members of Roots and Shoots work together on three main goals. They care for the environment. They care for animals. And they care for people in their communities.

Roots and Shoots members have found different ways to reach these goals. For example, they might clean up trash from beaches or forests. They might volunteer at a zoo. Or they might cook a meal for homeless families in their community.

More than 7,500 young people are members of Roots and Shoots. Groups have formed in schools, communities, and universities. They are making a difference in more than ninety countries around the world.

Jane meets children from all over the world through Roots and Shoots.

FURTHER READING

NONFICTION

Gogerly, Liz. *Dian Fossey.* Austin, TX: Raintree Steck-Vaughn, 2003. Read the story of Dian Fossey, another student of Louis Leakey. She became a gorilla expert.

Goodall, Jane. *The Chimpanzees I Love: Saving Their World and Ours.* New York: Scholastic Press, 2001. Jane describes her life with the chimpanzees in Gombe and her work to protect the animals.

Goodall, Jane. *With Love.* New York: North-South Books, 1998. Jane shares many stories about her chimpanzee friends in Gombe.

Kane, Karen. *Chimpanzees.* Minneapolis: Lerner Publications Company, 2005. Lots of color photos help readers learn about chimp talk, baby chimps, and dangers to chimps.

FICTION

Goodall, Jane. *Rickie and Henri: A True Story.* New York: Penguin Young Readers Group, 2004. This picture book is about a small chimpanzee who is rescued after a hunter kills her mother.

WEBSITES

Chimpanzees: National Geographic for Kids
http://www.nationalgeographic.com/kids/creature_feature/0112/chimps.html This website includes facts about chimpanzees as well as video and sound recordings.

The Jane Goodall Institute
http://www.janegoodall.org/ The institute's website includes information about Jane and the chimpanzees at Gombe.

Jane Goodall's Wild Chimpanzees
http://www.pbs.org/wnet/nature/goodall/ Learn more about Jane and see photographs of the chimpanzees she studied.

Roots & Shoots
http://www.rootsandshoots.org/ This is the official website of Jane's organization for children.

SELECT BIBLIOGRAPHY

BOOKS
Goodall, Jane. *Africa in My Blood: An Autobiography in Letters: the Early Years.* Edited by Dale Peterson. Boston: Houghton Mifflin, 2000.

Goodall, Jane. *Beyond Innocence: An Autobiography in Letters: the Later Years.* Edited by Dale Peterson. Boston: Houghton Mifflin, 2001.

Goodall, Jane and Phillip Berman. *Reason for Hope: A Spiritual Journey.* New York: Warner Books, 1999.

Lindsey, Jennifer. *Jane Goodall: 40 Years at Gombe.* New York: Stewart, Tabori & Chang, 1999.

Montgomery, Sy. *Walking with the Great Apes: Jane Goodall, Dian Fossey, Biruté Galdikas.* Boston: Houghton Mifflin, 1991.

VIDEO
Jane Goodall: My Life with the Chimpanzees. VHS. Washington, D.C.: National Geographic Society, 1990.

Reason for Hope: A Spiritual Journey. VHS. St. Paul: KTCA-TV, Twin Cities Public Television, 1999.

INDEX

Acknowledgments

For photographs and artwork: AP Photo/MTI, Barnabas Honeczy, p. 4; © National Railway Museum/SSPL/The Image Works, p. 7; © Steven May/Alamy, p. 8; © E.O. Hoppé/CORBIS, p. 10; National Archives, p. 11; © Tom Brakefield/SuperStock, p. 15; The Jane Goodall Institute, pp. 16, 35; © Dr. John Michael Fay/National Geographic/Getty Images, p. 20; Hugo van Lawick/The Jane Goodall Institute, p. 21; © age fotostock/SuperStock, p. 22; Bill Wallauer/The Jane Goodall Institute, p. 23; Derek Bryceson/The Jane Goodall Institute, p. 24; © Michael Nicholson/CORBIS, p. 25; PhotoDisc Royalty Free by Getty Images, p. 26; © Hugo van Lawick/National Geographic Society Image Collection, pp. 29, 34; AP Photo, pp. 30, 32; © Bettmann/CORBIS, p. 31; © Ann B. Keiser/SuperStock, p. 33; AP Photo/San Diego Union-John Gibbons, p. 38; © Peter Johnson/CORBIS, p. 39; © Henry Diltz/CORBIS, p. 40; AP Photo/Jean-Marc Bouju, p. 41; © Henny Ray Abrams/AFP/Getty Images, p. 43; AP Photo/M. Spencer Green, p. 45.
Front Cover: © Danita Delimont/Alamy. **Back Cover:** © age fotostock/SuperStock.
For quoted material: p. 10, Jennifer Lindsey, *Jane Goodall: 40 Years at Gombe* (New York: Stewart, Tabori & Chang, 1999); p. 17, Jane Goodall and Phillip Berman, *Reason for Hope: A Spiritual Journey* (New York: Warner Books, 1999).